Koala Books:

The Ultimate Koala Book for Kids

101 Koala Facts, Photos, Quiz and Word Search Puzzle

Jenny Kellett

Copyright © 2021 by Jenny Kellett
Cover image Photo from Freepik

Visit us at:
www.bellanovabooks.com

All rights reserved. No part of this book may be reproduced in any form by any electronic or mechanical means including photocopying, recording, or information storage and retrieval without permission in writing from the author.

ISBN: 9798708873804
Imprint: Independently published

Contents

Koala Facts 6
Koala Quiz 64
Quiz Answers 68
Word Search Puzzle 70
Sources 72

Introduction

Koalas have found their way into millions of hearts . They're oh-so-cuddly and ridiculously cute, so it's hard not to love these fluffy marsupials!

In this book you will learn lots of fun and interesting facts about koalas, then have a chance to test your new knowledge in our Koala Quiz.

Are you ready? Let's go!

A koala and joey.

Koala Facts

Although koalas look like bears, they are actually marsupials. Other marsupials include wombats and kangaroos.

• • •

What is a marsupial? Marsupials are mammals that give birth to not-quite developed young, and they are usually carried in a pouch. Most marsupials live in Australia and New Zealand. However, there are a few species in the Americas.

The scientific name for the koala is *Phascolarctos cinereus*.

• • •

Koalas can only be found in the wild in Australia. Specifically, in the southeastern and eastern areas of Australia — mostly along the coastlines.

• • •

Baby koalas are called 'joeys'.

• • •

Joeys develop in their mother's pouch for around six months. They spend the next six months hitching a ride on their mother's back.

A young grey koala.

A koala in Duncan, Australia.

Joeys use their mother's pouch for feeding and sleeping until they are one year old.

• • •

Koalas have a strict diet of just eucalyptus. They can eat over 1kg of leaves every day.

Koalas live high up in eucalyptus trees. Often you can see them wedged between the fork of tree branches eating or sleeping.

· · ·

Not all eucalyptus is good enough for the koala, though! There are over 700 species of eucalyptus, but koalas only eat around 50 of those.

· · ·

Eucalyptus is poisonous to most other animals, so koalas don't have much competition for food.

A koala doing what it does best.

Koalas don't get many nutrients from eucalyptus, which is why they usually sleep around 20 hours of the day!

• • •

Koalas are solitary creatures, and the only bonding that happens is between a mother and its joey and during mating.

• • •

Koalas can range in weight from 4-15 kg (9–33 lb). In general, koalas in northern habitats are smaller and lighter than those in the south.

Koalas can have a range of different fur colours, from silver-grey to a chocolate brown.

• • •

Koalas don't have many predators, however, they are at risk of a couple of serious diseases: Chlamydia and the koala retrovirus.

• • •

Chlamydia can devastate whole populations of koalas, and they are more likely to get the disease when they are stressed. Left uncured, the disease causes blindness and infections in their reproductive organs.

You can find cave paintings of koalas by Indigenous Australians from many millennia ago.

• • •

Koalas are listed as 'vulnerable' by the International Union for Conservation of Nature. In the early 20th century they were hunted heavily for their fur, but now they are protected.

• • •

The main threat to koalas is a loss of habitat. Large bushfires and deforestation destroy the eucalyptus trees they call home. Koalas are protected, but their habitat is not.

The name 'Koala' comes from the Aboriginal word meaning 'no water'. It was once believed that koalas didn't need to drink any water, but this was found to not be true. You can often see koalas coming down from the trees to search for water during hot weather and droughts.

...

Koalas do, however, get most of their water from their food. Eucalyptus leaves are 55% water.

...

Koalas have what is called a 'vestigial tail', meaning it is not visible, but there is still evidence of it on its skeleton.

Male koalas are 50% heavier than females. Male koalas also have more curved noses.

...

Male koalas have special scent glands on their chest. They use these to mark their presence, particularly when searching for a mate.

...

When a male koala is looking for a mate it lets out a very loud bellow that is designed to intimidate other males and impress females.

Koalas may be cute, but they're not so smart! They have one of the smallest brains in relation to its body weight of any mammal. Scientists believe that because they don't consume many nutrients, they can't support a larger brain size.

• • •

Their brains take up only 61% of the space inside their skulls.

• • •

Koalas don't have good eyesight. They have small eyes with vertical pupils, which is unusual among marsupials.

A young koala at Lone Pine Koala Sanctuary in Brisbane Australia.

Koalas sometimes store leaves in their cheeks before they are ready to chew and swallow it.

• • •

Sometimes koalas regurgitate their food so that they can eat it again.

• • •

Koalas eat so many leaves that they smell like eucalyptus! This also acts as a natural insect repellent.

Although koalas can swim, they often drown in swimming pools while looking for water to drink because they aren't able to lift themselves out. Australians who own a swimming pool are advised to provide a way for koalas to get to safety.

• • •

There is only ever one koala living on a tree.

• • •

Koalas are mostly nocturnal. This means they sleep during the day and are awake at night. However, koalas sometimes come out during the daytime too.

A sleeping koala at Kuranda Koala Gardens.

A very chilled koala at Australian Reptile Park.

The closest relative to the koala is the wombat!

• • •

Mating season for koalas is between November and February in southern populations, and from September to January in the north.

• • •

The gestation period (how long the mother is pregnant for) is only 35 days.

Koalas usually have one joey per year, but older koalas may only have one every two years.

• • •

When koalas are born they are about the size of a jellybean!

• • •

The lifespan of a koala is around 12 years in the wild and 16+ years in captivity.

Koalas have extra thick, wooly fur, which protects them from severe weather in the cooler winter months.

• • •

Koalas have rough pads on their hands and feet, which help them to grip while climbing.

• • •

Koalas have large noses with sensitive hairs, which are useful for sniffing out their food sources and checking the eucalyptus is good enough to eat.

As they don't have sweat glands, when a koala is hot it often licks itself to cool down.

• • •

In 2019-20, Australia had some of its worst-ever bushfires, and thousands of koalas died.

On Kangaroo Island, in South Australia, a veterinarian estimated that 30,000 koalas were killed in the bush fires there out of a population of 50,000.

A wild koala on the Great Ocean Road, Victoria, Australia.

There are many famous fictional koalas! Have you heard of Blinky Bill, Nigel from the Disney movie The Wild, or Bunyip Bluegum?

• • •

One of the most popular chocolates in Australia is called Caramello Koalas. These are small koala-shaped chocolates filled with caramel.

• • •

Many Australians trick tourists by telling them stories of the 'drop bear'. This fictional animal is based on the koala, and they are said to drop out of the trees and attack people as they walk past! Now you know, you can't be tricked :)

Koalas are very cuddly, and in many Australian zoos and sanctuaries, you have the opportunity to hold one. But watch out, their claws are sharp so sometimes they might accidentally scratch you!

• • •

Koalas feature in many Australian Aboriginal myths called Dreamtime stories. One myth from the Tharawal people tells of how koalas helped row the boat that brought them to Australia.

• • •

Early European settlers described the koala as having a "fierce and menacing look"! People certainly don't look at the koala that way anymore, though.

In 1983, Paul McCartney and Michael Jackson did a duet called "Ode to a Koala Bear".

• • •

In the state of Victoria, you can see the Giant Koala — a huge statue that attracts lots of tourists.

• • •

In the early 20th Century, millions of koalas were culled in Queensland. This caused huge anger among Australians and was the first large environmental controversy the country faced.

In the 1920s and 1930s, the first koala sanctuaries were built: Lone Pine Koala Sanctuary and Sydney's Koala Park Sanctuary.

• • •

Eucalyptus trees are also known as gum trees.

• • •

Although koalas prefer to live in quiet areas, they can survive perfectly well in urban areas as long as they have enough trees.

• • •

It is illegal to keep a koala as a pet.

Koalas are herbivores, this means they only eat plants.

• • •

Koalas have a very long digestive organ called the caecum, which helps them to digest the tough eucalyptus leaves. While humans, and many other animals, have a caecum, the koala's is around 2 metres long!

• • •

The Australian Koala Foundation estimates that there are only around 80,000 koalas still living in the wild.

Koalas have five digits on each paw, two of which are opposable like human thumbs.

• • •

On their hind paws, the two opposable digits are fused together to create a grooming claw.

• • •

The area where koalas live is called a home range. Within this home range are several home trees — the trees that they eat from regularly. These home ranges can sometimes overlap with other koalas'.

Koalas communicate with each other using very strange sounds. One of the most common ones sounds like a loud snore and then a burp!

. . .

As eucalyptus leaves are toxic, young koalas must first feed on a substance called 'pap', which comes from its mother's poop. It contains micro-organisms, which prepare the joey's intestines to be able to handle its new diet. They feed on pap for around 6-7 weeks before coming out of their pouch.

When a joey reaches the age of between 1 and 3 years old, it leaves its mother's home range to find its own.

• • •

Female koalas are mature when they reach 2 years of age. Male koalas mature a little later — at around 3 or 4 years.

• • •

As different types of eucalyptus grow in different states, the diet of a koala in Queensland is very different from one in Victoria.

Koalas can only absorb about 25% of the fibre that they eat, which is one of the reasons why they have to eat so many leaves!

• • •

You can often see koalas hugging trees. Scientists discovered that this is to help them stay cool! When the weather gets hot, koalas move to lower parts of the tree and press themselves up close to find the coolest spots.

• • •

Koalas fingerprints are almost identical to that of a human! The only difference is that koalas have warts on their hands and feet.

Koalas are the only animals other than primates that have fingerprints.

• • •

Koalas also have unique patterns on their noses, which help biologists to identify them.

• • •

Although rare, white and albino koalas do exist. An albino koala was born at San Diego Zoo in 1985, it was white with a pink nose and eyes.

Koalas may seem slow, but if necessary they can run up to 32 km/h (19.8 mph)! They can also jump 2 metres up a tree if frightened.

• • •

Wild koalas are declining at a rate of 53% in Queensland, 26% in the small remaining population of New South Wales and 14% in Victoria. This is why they are on the Vulnerable list.

• • •

On May 3rd every year in Australia it is National Wild Koala Day. The day is used to raise awareness about koalas and their shrinking habitat.

A koala at Currumbin Wildlife Sanctuary. Credit: Nghia Nguyen

Despite many large areas seeing a decline in koalas, there are some places that are overpopulated with koalas! These include French Island, Kangaroo Island and Raymond Island. Many koalas in these areas are relocated to less populated areas.

...

While koalas may look cuddly, they feel very stressed if humans are nearby. They will even bite and scratch if they feel threatened. It is best to keep a distance of 10 metres from a koala in the wild, so as not to scare it.

Koalas have a section of strong cartilage at the end of their spine, which helps them sit comfortably for long periods of time in trees.

• • •

Ironically, considering the country where they live, koalas are better prepared for surviving in cold weather than in warm weather thanks to their thick fur.

• • •

Koalas have pouches that open at the rear. This is unusual in marsupials, and it also means that koalas need strong muscles to be able to stop their young from falling out of the pouch! This is different from the kangaroo, which has an upward-opening pouch.

• • •

Koalas are warm-blooded. This means that they maintain consistent body temperature, slightly above its natural surroundings. Their body temperature is 36.6°C (97.88°F).

• • •

While we know them as the Koala, Indigenous Australians have many other names, including *Kaola, Koalo, Koolewang, Koobor, Colah, Coola* and *Cullawine.*

Koala babies can also have different names beside joeys, including "pouch young", "back young", and "cubs" depending on their age and development stage.

• • •

Koalas have few predators but have been known to be taken by dingoes and large owls. The young are also at threat from eagles and other animals.

• • •

The word 'marsupial' comes from the Latin word marsupium, meaning 'pouch'.

Koalas have a white speckled patch of fur on their bums, which makes them harder to detect from the ground.

• • •

Koalas have a very well developed sense of smell, which helps them to identify eucalyptus leaves that are too toxic for them to eat.

• • •

The koala's sense of smell is developed as soon as it is born, which is what helps the newborn joey find its way through the pouch and onto its mother's teat to drink milk.

Once a joey finds its mothers teat, the teat expands inside its mouth to keep the newborn in place.

• • •

A female koala is often called a 'doe', while a male koala is called a 'buck'.

• • •

Koala's rib cages only have 11 rib pairs, which is the least of any other marsupial.

Koalas have a resting heart rate of 70-140 beats per minute, however, it can be hard to measure as they have a 'sinus arrhythmia', meaning their heart rate and breathing can be out of sync.

• • •

You should never pick a koala up from its underarms like you would a cat or baby. They aren't used to being touched in this area, so it makes them uncomfortable.

• • •

Koalas have a curved spine, which gives them their famous pear shape. This makes it easier for them to curl into trees.

Koalas' fur has a waterproof shield to protect them in rainy weather.

• • •

75 per cent of tourists to Australia said that seeing a koala was top of their must-see animals' list!

Koala Quiz

Now test your knowledge in our Koala Quiz! Answers can be found on page 67.

1. Where does the name 'koala' come from?

2. Koalas only eat eucalyptus leaves. True or false?

3. Where can you find koalas in the wild?

4. What is the koalas closest relative?

5. What is a baby koala called?

6. When does a baby koala first leave its mother's pouch?

7. What is the main threat to koalas today?

8. Which sense is the best developed in koalas: sight or smell?

9. How many hours a day do koalas sleep?

10. How long is a koala pregnant for?

11. What type of animal is a koala?

12. Where do koalas get most of their water from?

13. Koalas are larger and heavier in the northern or southern populations of Australia?

14. How big is a joey when it's born?

15. Koalas have fingerprints. True or false?

16. What do koalas have that helps them sit comfortably in trees for long periods of time?

17. How many koalas live in a single tree?

18. How long do koalas live for?

19. What is the name of the substance joeys eat from their mothers to protect themselves from toxic eucalyptus leaves?

20. At what age do koalas leave their mother's home range to find their own?

Answers:

1. From the Aboriginal word meaning 'no water'.
2. True.
3. In eastern and south-eastern Australia, mostly along the coast.
4. The wombat.
5. A joey.
6. Around six months old.
7. A loss of habitat.
8. Smell.
9. Up to 20!
10. 35 days.
11. A marsupial.
12. Eucalyptus leaves.
13. The south.
14. About the size of a jellybean.
15. True.
16. Strong cartilage at the bottom of their curved spines.
17. Just one.
18. 12 years in the wild and 16+ yeras in captivity.
19. Pap.
20. Between 1-3 years old.

KOALAS
WORDSEARCH

A	F	G	H	J	F	D	S	A	N	U	I
M	V	U	L	N	E	R	A	B	L	E	D
K	O	A	L	A	B	F	D	S	D	U	S
T	Y	E	F	D	S	S	P	O	U	C	H
F	N	B	D	A	G	E	G	F	D	A	F
L	M	A	R	S	U	P	I	A	L	L	E
U	T	E	K	K	M	R	T	W	F	Y	W
F	R	F	J	B	T	R	E	W	G	P	A
F	A	U	S	T	R	A	L	I	A	T	N
Y	G	H	D	R	E	G	F	D	H	U	B
G	H	D	J	O	E	Y	R	F	E	S	R
A	D	F	H	J	R	D	A	G	S	F	D

Can you find all the words below in the wordsearch puzzle on the left?

KOALA   EUCALYPTUS   MARSUPIAL

JOEY   GUM TREE   POUCH

AUSTRALIA   VULNERABLE   FLUFFY

Sources

"10 Koala-Ty Facts About Koalas". 2018. Wwf.Org.Au. https://www.wwf.org.au/news/blogs/10-interesting-facts-about-koalas#gs.gczysv.

Logan, M. (2001). "Evidence for the occurrence of rumination-like behaviour, or merycism, in the koala (Phascolarctos cinereus, Goldfuss)". Journal of Zoology. 255 (1): 83–87. doi:10.1017/S0952836901001121

"Koala Express: Amazing And Interesting Facts About The Australian Koala.". 2020. Koalaexpress.Com.Au. https://www.koalaexpress.com.au/facts1.ht

South Australia's iconic Kangaroo Island could see rare species wiped out after devastating bushfires ABC News, 8 January 2020. Retrieved 13 September 2020.

"Frequently asked questions (FAQs)". Australian Koala Foundation. Archived from the original on 30 April 2013. Retrieved 21 September 2020.

"Interesting Facts | Australian Koala Foundation". 2020. Savethekoala.Com. https://www.savethekoala.com/about-koalas/interesting-facts.

"10 Things You Didn'T Know About Koalas". 2014. Mentalfloss.Com. https://www.mentalfloss.com/article/59114/10-things-you-didnt-know-about-koalas.

"Albino Koala Born At Zoo". 1985. Los Angeles Times. https://www.latimes.com/archives/la-xpm-1985-10-20-me-14053-story.html.

Duffy, Janine. 2020. "Are Koalas High? 5 Biggest Myths About Koalas | Echidna Walkabout Tours". Echidnawalkabout.Com.Au. https://www.echidnawalkabout.com.au/are-koalas-high-5-biggest-koala-myths/#:~:text=A%20koala%20can%20run%20on,tree%20in%202%20metre%20bounds.

Planted, One. 2020. "11 Reasons To Celebrate Koalas On Wild Koala Day". One Tree Planted. https://onetreeplanted.org/blogs/stories/world-koala-day.

"Physical Characteristics Of The Koala | Australian Koala Foundation". 2020. Savethekoala.Com. https://www.savethekoala.com/about-koalas/physical-characteristics-koala.

We hope you learnt some awesome facts about koalas!

Visit us at www.bellanovabooks.com for the latest book releases.

Printed in Poland
by Amazon Fulfillment
Poland Sp. z o.o., Wrocław
06 April 2021

8cf34791-383c-4518-94dd-341f03f28f51R01